# Lines to the Lost

Harvey Sagar

Published by Harvey Sagar 2015

Copyright throughout; all rights reserved

ISBN  978-0-9575537-8-1

Other works by the author include:

1. *Teddy Bear's Triumph: Tales from a Medical Allotment*

2. *DRY Out!*

3. *Come Rhyme With Me*

www.harveysagararts.com

To Jessica

## Contents

|  | Page |
|---|---|
| An Occasion to Say Goodbye | 6 |
| Reflections | 8 |
| At the Coast | 10 |
| Awakening | 12 |
| She Appears to Have Gone | 14 |
| I Stood Beside a Deep Lake | 16 |
| Nighttime | 18 |
| My Week | 20 |
| Not The End | 21 |
| Cancer | 22 |
| New Year's Eve | 24 |
| Walking | 26 |
| The Darkness | 28 |
| To One Gone | 31 |
| I Wish I Could Cry | 32 |
| You Can Stare at the Wall | 34 |

|  | **Page** |
|---|---|
| You Cannot Take It Away | 36 |
| Done in Style | 39 |
| Happy Memories | 40 |
| Next Year | 42 |
| Some People Say Death Is All Sad | 44 |
| My Choice Would Be a Coffin in Pink | 46 |
| Karen | 48 |
| Memories of a Daughter | 52 |
| Ups and Downs | 54 |
| Chagrin | 56 |
| Sacrifice | 59 |
| How Could God Do This to Me? | 60 |
| Christmas | 62 |
| Please Stay | 64 |
| The Past | 66 |
| Love | 69 |
| To One Dear | 72 |

## An Occasion to Say Goodbye

So now we've arrived at the funeral
For someone so loved and so beautiful;
An occasion to say goodbye to one gone;
An occasion to reflect and think on.

Members of family and friends are all here
To show love and respect for one dear,
One who by living enriched the ones left,
Who by dying leaves them lost and bereft.

Though our dearest may no longer be living,
Henceforward they still will be giving.
Through left memories, we share in their being
And in their spirit our souls they'll be seeing.

In partner, children, family and friends,
Stays a remnant that will never end.
A living body may no longer be here
But their presence will not disappear.

Our loved one has not lived in vain,

Though just now we feel lost in pain,

For their presence on earth left creation

Of a new life of hope, eternal bond and elation.

## Reflections

When all this is over and you reflect on the past,
Don't think what you should have done.
No-one has ever reversed what has gone;
Memories, what's left and the future live on.

You can blame yourself for not saying sorry
Or seeming to not care enough.
But it wasn't just you who hurt those they loved;
Quite frankly, life can be tough.

You can tell yourself, if you'd done this or that,
Then now things would surely be different.
But no-one is perfect; how we all wish that we were;
The worst is to be totally indifferent.

Please remember the good things, indeed as I do,
The times we enjoyed days together.
And also how we would somehow survive
Through the bad times, through all kinds of weather.

What I want you to do is to just carry on,
Live your life and, in peace, see it through.
And remember one thing which is quite simply this:
You love me and I'll always love you.

## At the Coast

At the coast, by the cliffs, on the sand-sheeted shores,
Where oystercatchers play in their random runs
And teasingly seals pop their heads through the waves:
There was our haven of fulfilment and fun.

In the spring, we saw whales and, on the cliffs, nesting falcons.
Walks on the coast path took us away from our cares;
And remember the storms, threatening winds, high waves crashing,
Giving invitations to come near to those who may dare.

We would often drive home, weather-beaten but laughing;
You would put on the coffee while I drowsed in a chair;
I could choose from a selection of your best homemade cakes,
Though sometimes I slept before I'd finished my share.

Back down at the beach, I still see those things.
The birds sing; the wind blows through my hair;
The tides, the surf, the sea life's not changed;
The one thing that's different is you're no longer there.

It's said, if you count, every seventh wave is the biggest.
One day, it seemed that wave wanted to speak;
It said it was strong but would die on the shore;
An image of boldness can soon become meek.

At the next seventh wave, the wind carried your voice.
It said, like the wave, you'd been faded and drained.
But then, as the swell petered out on the sand,
Reminded me strong waves would soon come again.

## Awakening

I awoke and saw you in the corner of the room
On a canvas of bright, golden light.
That moment dispelled all my feelings of gloom
As I saw that you were all right.

You were clothed in a dress of white cotton linen;
A smile was transfixed on your face.
You looked as if you wanted to listen;
Your demeanour was beauty and grace.

You had hair long and golden, eyes of deep powder blue;
Your right hand reached out in greeting.
I was so pleased you'd allowed me to see you
Though I sensed that the moment was fleeting.

I enquired where you'd come from but you did not reply;
You just gave me a look more intense.
I was desperate to ask you what, where and why
But I knew you would think it was nonsense.

And then you were gone; you left in a trice
But somehow a presence remained.
Can that beautiful memory completely suffice
To ease my long suffering pain?

## She Appears to Have Gone

She appears to have gone and, yes, you shed tears
For a life that you dreamed would go on for ever.
But which would she rather: live longer in pain
Or leave love and rich memories behind?

You can cry but would it bring her back?
You can wish that you could turn back the clock;
The words you said and those you didn't,
Regret will never change it all.

If only could have, would have, should have
Are words oft spoken but to no avail.
Today will always transform to tomorrow
And never become yesterday.

You can pray for her to return to the living;
You can ask that God will rework it all;
You can hope that something will rewind the clock
But you must know it's not going to happen.

What you can do is give praise for her living,
That the world is blessed by her being there at all;
That you'd rather she'd lived and you'd suffered pain
Than she had never existed at all.

One more thing you can do, if you're talking to God,
Is to admit that we don't understand
But keep faith that one day you'll be side by side,
Like eternal rainbows in a haven of love.

## I Stood Beside a Deep Lake

I stood beside a deep lake
By a dark mountain high;
I looked into the lake
And thought I saw your smile.

I asked you to come to the surface
And join me on the bank;
Then the water became covered
In a dull opaque mist.

I looked up but saw only dark;
Then a bright light appeared on the mountain.
Sun's rays criss-crossed o'er the summit
In a pattern that outlined your face.

You said don't gaze on the depths;
They are forbidding and empty.
Come and join me up here
And you will see the sunshine.

I'm asking you to climb the mountain
And I know that you will struggle.
But cherish each step upwards
And then you can share in my peace.

## Nighttime

The night nurse was kind as she tucked me up tight;
Her hair was dark auburn, her eyes blue and bright.
She said, "Come now, sleep; it's the end of the day."
Then she bid me goodnight though I wished she would stay.

The pains were not bad and I slept for a while;
I briefly awoke and thought of your smile;
I wanted to stay conscious to see if you'd come
But I started to hear distant drums.

The poet has said that no man is an island
And I seemed wandering alone in dark sea.
I was floating, desperate, looking for land
Until in a vision you came back to me.

I felt sure you weren't real as I stared at the deep;
I believed it was all in my mind
Until you held onto my hand and said, "Darling, sleep,
Now it's my turn to be kind."

You started to fade, a bright cloud upward lifting;
I still wondered if I was lost in a dream.
But soon I found my body was drifting
And then you said, "Please come with me."

In a pool at my feet were pearl oysters,
On a branch a bright cockatoo.
Music chimed down from heaven's cloisters;
I knew I'd be forever with you.

## My Week

On Monday, I will be down at the beach;
I'll see you there.
On Friday, I'll call at the charity shop;
I'll see you there.

On Saturday, I'll be down at the gym;
I'll see you there.
On Sunday, I will do TV and crosswords;
I'll see you there.

Each day, I'll drink tea and eat cakes,
Reflect on the memories we share;
The rest of the week, I am free;
I'll see you there.

## Not The End

So now it has happened; you've finally gone,
A long weary slide to the end;
The ups and the downs, the sadness and joy -
Now what does the future portend?

For so long, it seemed life could never go wrong;
We just basked in our love and our fun.
We were soul mates; we eased each other's pain;
By your side, I could just run and run.

You often gave me advice as the wise elder sister
And, in truth, I tried to take notice.
In return, I would always be there for your cares;
Why did they mistake your prognosis?

What I can say for sure is that nothing has changed
Except that your soul is not here.
But you're still the same girl whom I've loved with my heart
And your spirit remains dear - and near.

# Cancer

From that day I learned you had cancer,
All the days seemed to merge into one.
Each day, I would kiss you and hold you,
Knowing that, one day, you would be gone.

You said you felt fine and I think that you did;
You could always put on a smile.
I tried hard to share your emotions,
For us both to go one more mile.

Hospital visits, the consultant's words,
You absorbed as just one more day.
There was maybe once that you ventured to ask
How much longer did I think you would stay.

When your family and friends expressed their concerns,
You said that no-one should worry.
In a typical way, you would laugh, shrug and say
That you'd no plans to leave in a hurry.

But soon that's what you did, and you went somewhere else;
I asked then what we had left behind;
And the vision I saw was a bold, vibrant icon,
Unique, happy, loving and kind.

## New Year's Eve

In just over two hours, the new year will arrive,
When we can all celebrate the future.
Or reflect on the highlights of the previous twelve months
And, if we choose, the disasters and losses.

I lost my dear daughter, my wife lost her sister;
The world lost two wonderful people.
But they have both travelled to a beautiful country
And, in the sunshine, smile down on us here.

They both may think that last year was the worst
And I think all would surely concur.
But for them next year will be nothing but joy
While back here we dwell on the past.

If tomorrow they spoke to us, I know what they'd say:
They would wish us a happy new year.
But much more than that, they would point back to the past
To fond memories we never could lose.

They would ask us to cling on to things that will matter,
Not just in next year but for ever beyond.
They'd remind us that one day we will hug once again,
Meanwhile, keep close those on earth that we love.

So, when midnight arrives, they'd say raise a glass,
Not in sadness but positive pleasure
For lives unique, all love, irreplaceable
And two icons enthroned in eternity.

# Walking

You would walk with me over mountains;
We would trek for miles up the glens.
It may not now seem so easy
But do not give up on me now.

I know you think it's all over
But some endings are just a new start.
For ever, I am still walking with you;
I see you though you do not see me.

When you stop on the slopes for a breather,
And feel that you cannot go on,
Remember I'd say, "Few more steps to the top"
And I'm still here speaking to you.

At the summit, we'd stop for a picnic,
Gaze down at what we'd achieved.
Do the same now: climb to the finish
And enjoy the fruits of your trials.

You would walk with me over mountains;

We would trek for miles up the glens.

It may not now seem so easy

But do not give up on me now.

## The Darkness

Please speak before the night closes;
I need to hear your soft tones
Before the darkness imposes
And leaves me again all alone.

Will you ever return to my side?
Can I never again feel your joy?
Or are you for ever to hide,
Our presence together destroyed?

I believe you must be there somewhere;
I keep calling but get no reply;
Please ease me from this despair;
Don't let it be simply goodbye.

I hoped we'd be for ever together;
Your laugh would always ring in my ears.
Now I live in cold, stormy weather,
The rain matched by my constant, cold tears.

Please speak before the night closes;
I need to hear your soft tones
Before the darkness imposes
And leaves me again all alone.

## To One Gone

Although you don't speak, I know that you're there;
You're loving and praying with me.
Your presence each day relieves my despair;
My locked heart can then break out free.

I don't hear your bright voice or see your sweet face;
You just contact by some kind of touch.
You reach out from your place in the heavenly space
Just a little; but to me very much.

One day, something happened, your contact had gone;
I was left in the world on my own.
But I knew you'd come back if I only held on;
With your love I am never alone.

Please don't ever decide to leave me for good;
Don't let anything draw you away.
The world's trees would shatter into splinters of wood
And its rivers would sweep me away.

# I Wish I Could Cry

I wish I could cry like a fountain,
Gasp, tremble and holler out loud
But I'm held, imprisoned, immobile
Inside an oppressive dark cloud.

And where is that cloud's silver lining?
Where's the good that may offset the bad?
Just right now, I can see very little
Except a victim, broken and sad.

Every day, you drew out my love
For a creation unique on this earth.
Now the world seems hostile but empty;
No meaning, of hope a great dearth.

But I have to believe you'll be back
And we'll be together again,
Maybe not here in this wasteland
But in some idyll, with a purpose regained.

We'll hear the skies ringing with bells
And the seas will be colours of rainbows;
We'll be clothed in a warming, bright light,
Embraced in eternal repose.

I wish I could laugh like an idiot
Shriek, giggle and guffaw out loud;
One day, I will when we share a new life,
Reunited, adoring and proud.

## You Can Stare at the Wall

You can stare at the wall but your vision is blocked;
If you choose, you can look through the window.
You can close your ears and sit in silence
Or you can hear me talking to you.

Through the window, across the street and over the hills:
That's where you are likely to find me.
When you listen to people and share their concerns,
That's where you are likely to hear me.

I am here for you now as I have always been
And so just let us stay as we were.
I hold to my heart those who are now left behind;
Please cling on to memories dear.

But much more than that, let me stay in your life,
Not a body you can see, smell and feel,
But a loving spirit, always there by your side,
To help you move life to a level more real.

I don't need you to notice me or accept that I'm here
But I'll help you to decide what you do.
Look through the window and find those out there
Whom you love and, in return, will love you.

## You Cannot Take It Away

You can take away a child
But not take away her parents.
You can take away a spouse
But not take away a marriage.

You can take away a sister
But not take away a family.
You can take away a life
But not take away a memory.

You can take away a person
But not take away her friends.
You can take away a worker
But not take away her skills.

You can take away potential
But not take away achievement.
You can take a life long lasting
But not take away existence.

You can take away a body
But not take away a soul.
You can take away a man
But not take away a God.

You can take away life's pleasures;
You can take away day's hopes;
You can take away the closeness
But never take true love.

## Done in Style

No-one would doubt she always did things in style.
With such ease, the best tastes she'd embrace:
Designer clothes, her make-up just perfect,
Matching jewellery, no hair out of place.

She became instant friend to all whom she met;
She'd converse with all kinds of folk;
She'd listen to problems, provide her advice,
Consider what remedy she could invoke.

Her parties: the bubbly, canapes and fine wines!
Top hostess, conversationalist sublime;
A great sense of humour, her laugh not a chuckle,
But more like music with melody and time.

She could organise anything; indeed she had views,
Which it seemed always brought out the best.
I guess that if she could be here today
Her funeral arrangements she'd put to the test.

# Happy Memories

High waves, deep forests, pink flowers and snow,
Things that brought smiles to your lips;
Pistachios, bananas, good friends and bad jokes;
Vegetarian moussaka and chips.

Do you remember the time that we slept out one night
Under starlight beside a French lake?
We had no cover; you thought it was great;
For me, a massive mistake.

But we laughed as we did when your parents came round
For that family-based Christmas of fun.
The dinner was bliss and the games were just great
But the dog ate your Mum's raisin bun!

And do you recall your sister's wedding in Bath,
When your brother, such a serious best man,
Drank his way through the cocktails, the beer and the wine
And at midnight proposed to your nan?

I remember your laughter, the screams and the tears
When I forced you to do theme park rides.
I remember in Spain when we lay on the beach;
Your eyes fluttered in time with the tide.

Back then, it was real and now it's a memory,
One of many that sweep through my mind,
Every day of the week, every hour of the night,
Happy visions of a life left behind.

## Next Year

Next year will be better.
Yes, I know we've had funerals
But my red Christmas sweater
Was truly beautiful.

It's true we've felt sad
And lots of people have died.
But I have to feel glad
You sang carols and cried.

We missed those who'd gone
But Christmas dinner was yum.
And we did shed a tear
Before all that food filled my tum.

Their absence was felt
When we sat down to eat.
I had to loosen my belt,
Food that could not be beat.

The wine was first class
(And we drank to the lost),
Served in fine crystal glass,
No doubt at high cost.

As we sleep in our chairs,
We dream of those gone.
But we soon lose our cares
Until the world dawns.

## Some People Say Death Is All Sad

Some people say that death is all sad
But in some ways I'm feeling quite glad.
After the service, we get a good meal,
However despondent we feel.

Despite all the anguish, the crying and stress,
At least I can wear a new dress.
I thought I'd wear one in green, with blue shoes,
Those I wore on that great birthday cruise.

There'll be lots of drab dresses and men in black ties,
Clothing I'm now inclined to despise.
I will opt to wear a jumper in scarlet
And look like a vulgar street harlot.

After the funeral, I plan to drink brandy;
There's a pub near the crem that's quite handy.
After that, I will dance through the night
In the trust that you'll be all right.

Some kind person will carry me home;
If not, through the streets I may roam.
No doubt, I will have a jolly good night
But, in the morning, may not feel that bright.

Do you know why I'll do this? It's not I don't care
Because I know you would like to be there;
It was you who taught me, when one great thing is done,
Something new can bring yet more fun.

## My Choice Would Be a Coffin in Pink

My first choice would have been a coffin in pink
But the undertaker said it might create a bit of a stink.
When they offered me one in polished red cherry,
I felt like saying it's not a fruit we will bury.

For most of the time, the funeral director was kind
Though I was scared she might be reading my mind.
When I said you loved Thai food, she guessed in a trice
That my second choice was one made of boiled jasmine rice.

She unveiled all the options with the flair of a salesman:
"Now here is one with a personalised talisman;
Built of old oak, it survives in the roughest of grounds
And comes in, with inscriptions, at under five thousand pounds."

Next were the flowers; for you, I'd choose pansies
But the florist said they were hallmarks of dandies,
A term, I thought, was from some long bygone age
As she insisted much better would be hellibore and sage.

How boring is that? What's the point in just crying?
Even though we cannot escape from the dying?
Can it be that no-one has much fun anymore
And that even in death we must just gaze at the floor?

The one thing I know is that you would have parties
With loud music and women dressed up as tarties.
Even though it's you who has left us this day,
I know vibrant memories you would want here to stay.

## Karen

Karen was the first of the Medcalf congregation,
Which was soon to number two and later three and four.
Her sisters always viewed her with greatest admiration,
Fuelled with friendship, love, fun, empathy and more.

Complaints never feature much in her persona;
According to her, life is consistently fine.
Nobody could accuse her of being a moaner;
She has simply pursued a constant happiness line.

With Pippa, her sister, she went to a school
With a long name, abbreviated to JAGS.
She was head girl or deputy, encompassed the rules,
Quality uniform and designer school bags.

Her next step was finishing school in Geneva,
Which taught her French and maybe an awful lot more.
But love for her family and home didn't leave her
So she returned to work at Laycock and Shaw.

She learnt in that job to be a wine buff
And had inherited some good cooking genes.
With any raw produce, she'd cook some wonderful stuff;
Who knows what comes next? Maybe claret with beans?

She was wooed by a doctor with good looks and skills;
She and Steve have since made great partners-in-crime.
Like all marriages, they've had thrills, chills and bills
But can still make music that has melody and time.

Beautiful children, Jenny, Tessa and Joss,
All turned out intelligent, charming and funny.
In none of these children could you claim any loss,
Though, like all kids, their upbringing cost a fair sum of money.

For a family home, they chose an odd space,
Way down in the West in a county called Cornwall,
In a region with a strange name that is called Playing Place
Though admittedly with no graffiti on buildings or walls.

In that beautiful part of the world, they have settled,
Most certainly active and involved but not townies.
Steve's a well-known GP and for a lot more has mettle
And is lucky to come home to Karen's great brownies.

For her part, dear Karen devoted herself
To a job in society, working hard with Connections,
Caring for people who had lost love and wealth
And misplaced the benefit of strong drug injections.

Her smile is a comfort to all those around her;
She is always determined to keep strong and happy,
An aid to those who may struggle and flounder,
Like one of the few who can smile changing nappies.

Nobody could argue she makes the best lemon drizzle
And literally runs through life, best there could be.
Her exit will never be one great big fizzle;
She's even found time to plant a memorial tree.

## Memories of a Daughter

I remember your repeated cries of "Oh stuck"
When your trolley of bricks met an immoveable wall.
You were learning to walk and, by nature's grace,
You could speak before barely moving at all.

I remember we went out in the cold winter weather;
Your unique expression was even there at age three;
We built snow tables, chairs, knives, forks and spoons;
Your creative spirit just seemed to run free.

I remember you transfixed by the telly
In a parallel world down in Sesame Street.
I remember with your brother in the back of the car
Maurice and Doris tapes seemed to you such a treat.

I remember that after an outing you said thank you
And then asked if your brother had said thank you yet.
For years, you both engaged in that banter.
These icons of your childhood I will never forget.

When you were a teen, I took you to Liverpool;
You said there was a band you just had to see.
In the club, I jostled and learned about moshing
Though the music remained unfamiliar to me.

Later on, your favourite gear was Doc Martens;
You'd short skirts, bright make up, hair long and uncurled.
One day, you told me what you had discovered:
Nirvana was obviously the best band in the world.

But much more than this I remember a girl
Who in a dark world was sometimes alone.
But, when out of it, was simply a presence of joy
With humour, wit, kindness, now sadly all gone.

I will always remember the dearest of daughters;
I still can't believe that we must always part.
Our conversations, your creativity and sharpness of thought -
Your passing leaves a unique hole in my heart.

## Ups and Downs

When the baby cries, just change her nappy;
The child and you will then be happy
For you'll soon be able to get some rest,
While she sleeps soundly in her nest.

At the age of two, she won't be lazy
For she will just run round like crazy.
She'll start to talk and ask you questions
And not respond to your suggestions.

By the age of five, she's charming and bright
Except with her brother she may sometimes fight.
But never to worry: she's about to start school
And prove once again that she's really no fool.

For the next several years, your world she'll enchant
'Til she reaches fourteen and wants breast implants.
Adolescence may show her sullen and picky
And involvement in talking is sometimes quite tricky.

When the hormones have settled, an adult appears
And her latent good character continues for years.
She's charming, caring and constantly funny
Though she's still quite concerned for the size of her tummy.

But sometimes things do not go quite to plan
Though you remain at her side, her strongest dear fan.
She goes off on her own to ventures unclear
And you fret that soon she will end her career.

Now she is set all alone for the future;
No more can you truly her character nurture.
Events to unfold you can never foretell
But you just pray to God that all will go well.

In the end, she maintained her beliefs
That nowhere on earth would she get much relief.
She made her own choices, didn't much say,
But clearly, finally, did it her way.

## Chagrin

I desperately miss you but I'm also annoyed
That you'd swan off and leave a gaping great void;
That our love for you seemed to carry no weight,
That all of life's miseries at a stroke you'd inflate.

Could you really not hack it, really not sort it out?
Did you have to live years in destructive self-doubt?
And when meaning and happiness life seemed to forbid,
Did you have to escape it the way that you did?

Couldn't you hold fast to the memories we made?
Did the joy of your childhood totally lapse into shade?
What was it that made you forsake all your friends
And, when they upset you, not to just make amends?

Were you not proud of the things you achieved,
Of your humour, compassion and the works you conceived?
I'm so sad that you left it all without trace
Said, "I've had it, goodbye" - just so brazen-faced.

But I know none of that's true because I know you.
Through your dearest, kind heart something simply broke through;
The one who would never willingly hurt anyone
By some demon or illness was simply outdone.

## Sacrifice

If you had your time again,
Do you think that you'd still dare
To risk all your emotions
In a one-way traffic of care?

Would you give up half your mind
To a sacrificial love,
To one who could often take, not give,
In opinions, would not move?

Why stay to see them wreck a life
Yet help them in a mess?
Why not just remove yourself?
Why could you not care less?

When they suddenly left this earth
Well then, new life could start
With no more worries, no more tears,
Except for the broken heart.

## How Could God Do This to Me?

How can it be God could do this to me,
Take the one that I love in the cruelest of ways?
Did He do it on purpose or just close His eyes
Or when the world wreaked its havoc, diverted His gaze?

I prayed and I prayed for things to be different
But the pains and despair went on as they were.
I asked only for life to be a bit easier
But it seemed that my misery is what God preferred.

Did He see what was happening when my dearest fell ill?
Why was he not there when I expressed all my fears?
If he gives out His love for the whole of creation
Why does He ignore my non-coping and tears?

But then I remember a man on the cross,
Who, through rejection and anguish, struggled to see
Whether God was still by him or had left him to fate
Saying, "My God, why hast thou forsaken me?"

Yet despite feelings of loss, God raised him on high
And that holy man's influence can still now be seen.
This must give us a hope for our loved who have gone
That bright future will replace what has been.

Yes, I am angry and I don't understand
But a life that ends in just death has no point,
Unless we hold onto a certain belief
That one day God our souls will anoint.

## Christmas

So now we've arrived at Christmas Day,
Ten months since you decided no longer to stay.
As usual, we have turkey, stuffing, mulled wine,
Crackers, daft hats and decorations sublime.

It's sad you won't see them, at least not down here.
You'll miss your Mum's singing, the prosecco and beer.
You will not be there to win at charades
Or groan when someone says, "Why not play cards?"

Do you sense the atmosphere where you are sitting?
Do you feel that our party is really befitting
To one who decided to go somewhere else
And leave her family to cope by themselves?

But sadly one thing is sure and that is we miss you
Another is God says we will just see it through.
The celebrations down here without you are deafened
By those that accompany you up there in heaven.

## Please Stay

Don't go, I need you.
Please stay; I pray you.
You cannot leave;
My heart will grieve.

Stay, stay, stay;
Just one more try.
Live for the day,
Better by and by.

Think of the past,
Your Mum and Dad,
A love so vast,
The good and bad.

Your loving young brother,
Your friends who still call.
You are like no other;
Please don't forsake it all.

But that was a dream
And now it is past.
The world's best creations
Just don't seem to last.

## The Past

We talked and laughed and ran through fields;
We sorted out world's problems.
We joked how we could solve it all,
If only they would let us.

You were proud when you showed me your creations;
You were happy when I smiled.
You gave me a look of disbelief in yourself
When I said you had surpassed all ideals.

You gave love; you would care for all you might meet
Except perhaps for yourself.
Is there anyone here who would speak against you
Saving only that person herself?

We photographed sunflowers and kicked up the surf;
You never cried on the white-knuckle rides.
You cuddled our dog when he ploughed up the turf.
How I wish I could turn back the tide.

Why did you leave me when this world was your place?
Could my love really not make you stay?
Now you've departed and not left a trace
Except tomorrow to be yesterday.

## Love

Love hurts no-one except those who care;
Those who are willing to risk;
Those whose other's trials they may share;
Those prepared to see loss.

Love cries out loud for those who can hear
And laughs with those who can smile.
It holds back the feelings of fear
That one day its dearest are gone.

But when things go bad, it shares in the tears
And shines on the people who grieve.
It remains steadfast for days, months and years,
For the past and forever henceforth.

You cannot remove it for it refuses to go;
It will always be there at your side.
In all the days forward, just this you need know:
That Love will be living with you.

*And finally, for the living*

*(To Alastair)*

## To One Dear

Remember this, even when I have gone,
That for you the whole world could be won;
But never take roads that just make you sad
And, for what you have, just be glad.

Yes, take risks but be prepared to lose
And show caution in what you may choose.
If you win, then share with others elation;
If you lose, don't suffer deflation.

Enjoy every day with those whom you love;
Your life is a big treasure trove.
But it's sadly not just there for the taking;
The happiness is there for your making.

Like me, you may wonder if God's by your side
And sometimes His love seems to hide.
But one day I believe He will make it all clear
When we're reunited with those we hold dear.

So carry on upwards and just seize the day;
You have close family and friends who will stay.
Keep going, live, love and see it all through
And always remember be nothing but you.

www.ingramcontent.com/pod-product-compliance
Lightning Source LLC
Chambersburg PA
CBHW060703030426
42337CB00017B/2734